I WANT TO BE . . . Book Series
Creator/Producer: Stephanie Maze, Maze Productions
Writer and Educational Consultant: Catherine O'Neill Grace
Designer: Lisa Lytton-Smith

Photographers for I WANT TO BE A DANCER:
Sisse Brimberg, Catherine Karnow, Nicole Bengevino, Barbara Ries,
Annie Griffiths Belt, Richard T. Nowitz, Steve Mellon, Joan Marcus,
Joe McNally, Karen Kasmauski, Joel Sartore, Paul Kolnik, Johan Elbers

Other books available in this series:
I WANT TO BE AN ASTRONAUT
I WANT TO BE AN ENGINEER
I WANT TO BE A VETERINARIAN

Copyright © 1997 by Maze Productions
Photography credits appear on page 48.

Library of Congress Cataloging-in-Publication Data
Maze, Stephanie.
I want to be a dancer/by Stephanie Maze and Catherine O'Neill Grace.
p. cm.—(I want to be . . . book series)
Summary: Provides an overview of the many types of dance that exist
and describes what is involved in becoming a dancer.
ISBN 0-15-201299-0
1. Dance—Vocational guidance—Juvenile literature. [1. Dance—
Vocational guidance. 2. Vocational guidance. 3. Occupations.]
I. Grace, Catherine O'Neill, 1950– . II. Title. III. Series.
GV1597.M39 1997
792.8'023—dc20 96-21839

First edition
A C E F D B

Pre-press through PrintNet
Printed and bound by Tien Wah Press, Singapore

ACKNOWLEDGMENTS

We wish to thank the following people, companies, and institutions for their very valuable contributions to this book: Jim Sohm, Administrative Manager, San Francisco Ballet School, San Francisco; Michelle Mathesius, Chairperson, Dance Department, La Guardia High School of Music, Art, and the Performing Arts, New York; Dance Theatre of Harlem; Alvin Ailey American Dance Theatre; Eva F. Maze; Ruthe Stein; Thomas K. Walker, Graf-x, New York; A & I Color Laboratory, Los Angeles.

Many thanks, also, to the very talented people who have participated in the I WANT TO BE . . . project: the photographers; writer Catherine O'Neill Grace and designer Lisa Lytton-Smith; as well as our colleagues at Harcourt Brace Children's Books, publisher Louise Howton Pelan and editor Karen Weller-Watson, whose guidance has been invaluable.

And finally, our heartfelt gratitude to all the professionals in this book for allowing us to interrupt their busy schedules and for agreeing to be the wonderful role models children can look up to for many years to come.

To all children who dream the impossible dreams

Where to Start

Dance! It's something everyone can do—from toddlers to grandmothers, first graders to teenagers. All over the world, from New York City theater stages to nomads' campsites in Africa, people dance. They dance when they're happy; they dance when they're sad. They dance to worship, to celebrate, or to entertain. They dance to express their ideas and their feelings.

Although you don't have to be a professional to dance, you can be a professional dancer. At right, members of the professional dance troupe Bill T. Jones/Arnie Zane & Company perform. The dancers in this troupe come from several ethnic backgrounds and are an unusual mix of ages and physical sizes.

Bill T. Jones, the company's choreographer, has a reputation for creating dance pieces that are surprising, even shocking. A choreographer is an artist who designs dance steps and sets them to music or sound. Jones started out in college as a film student, but he soon turned to dance to express his ideas. He found dance more poetic and more direct than filmmaking. As he told a dance writer for the *New York Times*, "My muscles understood it, and my heart and mind followed."

Do your muscles, heart, and mind urge you to be a dancer? As you read this book, you will learn that there are different paths to a career in dance—and different types of this vital art form to learn along the way. Shall we dance?

Types of Dance

When people say they have seen dance, they often mean classical ballet, an art form that began in Italian royal courts of the fifteenth century. Classical ballet has been the core of professional dance for hundreds of years and remains very popular today. In the large picture at left, dancers Susan Jaffe and Victor Barbee of the world-famous American Ballet Theatre perform a *pas de deux*—a piece for two dancers—in the ballet *Gaieté Parisienne*.

Of course, classical ballet, with its precise movements and formal poses, is not the only type of dance. Far from it. Dance is an art that has changed continuously through the centuries. Dancers keep trying new things. For example, contemporary dance can be wild and acrobatic, like the quick flip an Aerodance troupe member performs (far left, bottom). Dance can express deep emotion, like the graceful piece *Lovers* performed by members of the Jennifer Muller Dance Company (far left, top). Modern dance began in the early twentieth century. It was developed by choreographers who wanted to give dancers more room for individual style and expression than they thought the formal style of classical ballet allowed.

Traditional ethnic or folk dances—like the Native American dance being performed during a powwow in Texas (top left)—are as old as the tribes that created them. Today many Native Americans learn their tribal dances to honor their ancestors and to keep their cultures alive. Dance keeps countries' national pride alive, too, like the performances of the vibrant Ballet Folklórico Nacional de México, shown in the large photo on the next two pages.

Can you imagine yourself in any of these pictures? What about ballroom dancing (bottom left)? This whirling couple is taking part in a ballroom dance competition at Christmastime.

Moving current. *A quartet of Dance Theatre of Harlem dancers (above left) represents moving water in a ballet called* The River. *Founded in 1968 by former New York City Ballet dancer Arthur Mitchell as a tribute to Dr. Martin Luther King Jr., Dance Theatre of Harlem has performed to rave reviews all over the world. Its style is neoclassical. Meow!* CATS *(above right)—a smash-hit show based on poems by T. S. Eliot—opened in London in 1981 and has been popular ever since. The dance steps were choreographed by Gillian Lynne, who gave each cat character its own distinctly feline way to move around the stage.*

Tap time. *Top-hatted dancers (above left) strut their stuff in the musical* My One and Only, *choreographed by Tommy Tune. The show pays tribute to an American tradition: tap dancing. Dance historians say that tap dancing, like jazz, grew out of African rhythms brought to North America by slaves. Rock on. At a benefit performance for the City Kids Foundation, an urban arts program in New York, superstar Paula Abdul (above right) sings and shows off her energetic, athletic dance style. Rock-and-roll concerts and rock videos continue to introduce vibrant new types of dance to the world.*

The San Francisco Ballet School

Founded in 1933, the San Francisco Ballet is America's oldest ballet company. Some of the young dancers on these pages, students at the San Francisco Ballet School, will grow up to join and play starring roles in the historic company. Others may not make it, even if they work long and hard.

Ballet is a difficult, demanding art form. Competition starts early. The students on these pages had to pass an audition before they were admitted to the school. To succeed as a ballet dancer, you need dedication, good training beginning at an early age, a strong and flexible body, lots of talent—and a little luck. The San Francisco Ballet School accepts students starting at age seven. The school looks for children who have "an ear for music and an instinct for movement."

Any of the young dancers stretching out at the barre and on the studio floor (above) would tell you that although it's hard work, learning ballet is fun!

In class, dancers-in-training wear simple leotards and tidy hairstyles. That way, they can move easily, and the teacher can see exactly how they are holding their bodies and heads. This is

important because classical ballet consists of a vocabulary of formal steps and foot and arm positions.

In ballet, the way you hold your body is very important. You should always look light and lifted. Your body position is called your *placement,* which means the same in both French and English. French has been the language of ballet ever since the dance form became popular as entertainment at the court of Louis XIV of France in the seventeenth century.

As you practice and grow stronger, you learn more and more complicated movements and combinations of movements. Before long you're doing *ronds de jambe*—semicircular movements of the leg—or even *arabesques,* poses on one leg with the other leg extended gracefully behind you. You learn jumps, including *pas de chats,* which means "cat steps" in French, and *sissonnes,* jumps executed by leaping into the air with both feet off the ground. You also learn to *pirouette,* or "turn," without getting dizzy.

Eventually all the positions, steps, jumps, and turns that you repeat and repeat and repeat in class come together into a dance. You're moving gracefully across the stage. You're a ballet dancer!

A typical day at school. *Students at the San Francisco Ballet School stretch at the barre and on the studio floor (left). Above, from left, Sonia Evers, Hadley Suter, and Anise Gold-Watts fix their hair before class. Below, far left, Crystal Akimoto demonstrates a position with arms en haut, or "up high."*

A little higher. *At left, instructor Antonio Castilla adjusts the leg position of student John Vuong as his classmates practice. Below, Ariel Vitale concentrates on his arm position.*

Show time! *Dance students at Fiorello H. La Guardia High School warm up (top right), relax during a technical rehearsal (top left), and then pull themselves together beautifully for a full-fledged performance (middle left). In Washington, D.C., Moving Forward, a troupe of Asian American dancers, performs a dance that conveys the*

Other Education

If you try out a few dance steps in the hallways of your school, a teacher may ask you to stop. But at schools that offer special programs in the arts, dancing in the halls is perfectly acceptable behavior. Jessica Uzzan, shown in the large photo striking a flamenco pose in the hallway at Stuyvesant High School in New York City, has been dancing since she was four. Flamenco is a traditional, rhythmic style that developed from dances of Spanish gypsies. Jessica has displayed her talent by performing with the student branch of Ballet Hispanico, a New York City professional dance company.

At another New York City high school, student dancers give performances as part of their schoolwork. The dance department at Fiorello H. La Guardia High School of Music, Art, and the Performing Arts sponsors showcase days and holds senior dance concerts at graduation time. Many of the dance teachers at La Guardia have been performers with prominent dance companies such as the Joffrey Ballet, so they know the challenges—and the thrills—involved in putting on a show. The popular movie *Fame* and the television show based on it were modeled on what life is like for the aspiring dancers, musicians, and actors at La Guardia High.

At The Juilliard School, also in New York, students train in ballet and modern techniques in a demanding four-year, college-level course of study. The young dancers in the bottom photo at the far left are taking part in a modern jazz class there. Students also learn tap, choreography, acting, stagecraft, and much more. Juilliard graduates have joined established dance companies all over the world.

experience of immigrating to the United States. The company also offers workshops to young dancers, like those shown at bottom right.

Experience and Training

Ask almost any young dancer to name a ballet they have performed in—or would like to appear in—and you're likely to hear, *"The Nutcracker!"* Every Christmas season, amateur and professional dance companies perform this wonderful children's story. Based on a story by German fantasy writer E. T. A. Hoffmann, *The Nutcracker* features stirring music by Pyotr Ilich Tchaikovsky, magical mice, toy soldiers that come to life, a Christmas tree that grows to dizzying heights, a series of impressive solos, *pas de deux,* trios and quartets that show off dancers' most spectacular moves—and lots of small children.

Because there are so many parts, the ballet offers even very young dancers a wonderful opportunity to perform. Ballet training is difficult and demanding, so getting to show off what you've learned is a real treat! As a teenager, Chelsea Clinton, the president's daughter and a ballet student, appeared in a *Nutcracker* production. She danced with the Washington Ballet, which runs a company and a ballet school in Washington, D.C.

The pictures on these pages show the Washington Ballet preparing for its annual *Nutcracker* production. The excited young dancers lined up giggling (top) are about to try out for parts as mice. The more serious dancers (center) will audition for roles as toy soldiers.

Nutcracker season. *The photos on these pages, all of the Washington Ballet in Washington, D.C., show the hard work—and fun—of putting on a production of the beloved ballet, from performing onstage, to observing what goes on backstage.*

Almost ready. *Soldier makeup goes on for a dress rehearsal (bottom far left). In uniform, the troop is ready to march onstage (top). A young ballerina checks her toe shoe (above left), while another is fitted with her dress for the party scene in the first act (above right).*

Onstage Experience

Appearing onstage in *The Nutcracker* gives young dancers a chance to share the spotlight with professionals, who dance the major roles. In the large picture at right, a group of dancers—or *corps de ballet*—performs in a lavish New York City Ballet production of *George Balanchine's The Nutcracker*™. In the smaller photos, professionals from the New York Dance Theatre (top right), the Joffrey Ballet (second from top), and the New York City Ballet (third from top) work with amateur dancers. Two young aspiring ballet stars from the School of American Ballet perform a graceful *pas de deux* (bottom right).

George Balanchine's The Nutcracker™ tells the story of a magical toy that a little girl, Marie, receives for Christmas. She falls asleep and all kinds of magical adventures begin. The toy nutcracker turns into a prince, who leads Marie to the Land of Sweets, where his subjects—including Mother Ginger and her puppets, called Polichinelles (third inset from top)—dance for them. Is it all a dream? We can't be sure.

The Nutcracker premiered in St. Petersburg Russia, in 1892, and for more than a century the ballet has been enchanting audiences both young and old. Many famous dancers, such as Rudolf Nureyev and Mikhail Baryshnikov, have performed in it and adapted new versions for the stage. Maybe you will dance in *The Nutcracker* someday or create a new version of it!

Did You Know . . .

. . . that by 1996 there had been more than 3,300 performances of *Grease* on Broadway? The swirling, twirling jitterbuggers at right appeared in a 1995 production of the show directed by Tommy Tune.

. . . that the United States government attempted for many years to outlaw Native American dancing? The law that labeled tribal dancing an offense was not repealed until 1934.

. . . that modern dancer Martha Graham, who died at age ninety-two in 1991, created almost two hundred dances in her lifetime and continued to perform when she was in her seventies?

. . . that toe shoes weren't used in ballet until Maria Taglioni introduced them in 1832 when she danced the romantic *La Sylphide* in Paris?

. . . that contemporary dance performances have happened in some unusual places, such as in a full swimming pool, on the beach, and at a roller-skating rink?

. . . that the oldest ballet still being performed, *The Whims of Cupid and the Ballet Master,* was choreographed in 1786 for the Royal Danish Ballet, which has staged the comic dance ever since?

. . . that Anna Pavlova, a world-famous Russian dancer whose signature piece was "The Dying Swan," introduced ballet to Australia, India, Japan, and South America in the early 1900s?

. . . that the Russian Bolshoi Ballet has some three hundred dancers in its company? You probably won't be surprised to learn that *bolshoi* means "big" in Russian!

. . . that Pilobolus—a troupe founded by students at Dartmouth College in New Hampshire who combine mime, gymnastics, and dance—is named after a farmyard fungus that thrives on light?

Dance-Related Careers

You may love the drama, the costumes, the excitement of dance but have a hard time imagining yourself onstage. Don't worry. Performing isn't the only way to be involved in the world of dance.

In the pictures on these pages, various dance professionals create magic. For some, like musicians Mary Tryer, a harpist, and Edgardo Malaga, a bass player, accompanying a Washington Ballet performance of *The Nutcracker* (top right), the magic is musical. Other professionals create an enchanting atmosphere for dance with stage light. That's what lighting designer Maureen Tobin—shown working at a computerized light board (center right)—is doing. Her skill with stage lighting makes *The Nutcracker* set look mysterious and beautiful, and highlights the Washington Ballet dancers' skills.

Some dance professionals may never stand in a spotlight. But they bring the magic of dance into the lives of people who really need it. At bottom right, dance therapist Jenna Kipp works with an elderly resident of a nursing home. Kipp's dancing can bring people out of depression and loneliness and helps them express their feelings without using words. Dance therapists work with the elderly, with people who have mental illnesses, and with children who have disabilities. Kipp was trained in dance and movement and studied psychology, too. Dance therapists use movement to help patients heal.

Behind the scenes. *Makeup artist Anne Salt puts finishing touches on the face of New York City Ballet dancer Amanda Edge (top left). Director of costumes Holly Hynes adjusts Michelle Gifford's skirt (top center). Dance instructor Jacqulyn Buglisi checks student Sumayah McRae's posture in a class at The Juilliard School, in New York City (top right). Kevin McKenzie, a principal dancer turned artistic director at the American Ballet Theatre, coaches soloists Amanda McKerrow and Angel Correa in a rehearsal of the ballet* Le Corsaire *(bottom left). Modern dance choreographer Merce Cunningham works on a dance movement with a member of his dance company (bottom right).*

A Day at the National Dance Institute

Jacques d'Amboise believes that dance is for *all* kids, and he proves it over and over again at the National Dance Institute in New York City.

For thirty-two years d'Amboise was a principal dancer with the New York City Ballet. He was performing as a soloist at age seventeen. When he left the stage, d'Amboise began living out his dream: to teach kids in the city where he grew up to dance. He founded the National Dance Institute in a spare space of his son's school in 1976.

Since then the NDI has grown by leaps and bounds. The institute has five choreographers among its staff of thirty-one, runs exchange programs with Russia and China, puts on a big annual production involving hundreds of young dancers, and holds summer workshops such as the one shown in these photos. Here, New York public school students take classes and rehearse with teacher Lori Klinger (above and top photos, facing page) for a final outdoor performance at the World Financial Center in New York City (right). During the school year, the NDI offers classes in New York and throughout the country.

Dancers who work with d'Amboise may not

go on to join the big ballet companies, but that's not really the point of the program. Many of the young people d'Amboise and his staff work with come from very tough neighborhoods. Jacques d'Amboise understands those kids, because *he* grew up in a tough neighborhood. He knows that learning dance can help young people develop self-confidence and find purpose in their lives—as he did.

Summer Programs

If the kids on these pages were assigned an essay entitled "What I Did During Summer Vacation," they'd have a lot to say. These teenagers performed *Hello, Dolly!* at the Summer Musical Theater Workshop in Washington, D.C., and it was hard work to stage the musical comedy, which includes many song-and-dance numbers. In musical theater, dance helps tell the story. Its choreographers use a lively variety of dance styles, including ballet, modern, jazz, tap, and even acrobatics.

Show time at last, and Roxi Trapp-Dukes applies makeup backstage before dress rehearsal (above). At top right, choreographer Michael Bobbie helps dancers (from left) Caleb Gonzales, Rachel Shuler, Chris Ayer, and Molly Kierein get their posture exactly right for the number "We've Got Elegance." During a performance (center right), Rachel Rausch sings a solo as the leading character, Dolly Levi. In the photo at bottom right, the boys' ensemble belts out the show-stopping tune "Hello, Dolly!"

Summer dance camps and programs throughout the country offer young people who want to be dancers the luxury of concentrating on their art full-time. Participating in such a program is a great way to find out if you have the energy and dedication it takes to become a professional performer.

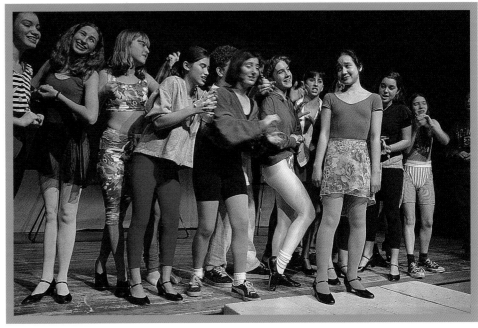

Time to dance. *The Rocky Mountains are an inspiring view for young dancers at Ballet West, a summer dance school in Snowmass, Colorado (top). These three ballet dancers are warming up at a barre in an open-air dance tent. In the photos above (left and right), students involved in the Capitol Area School for the Arts, an after-school program for thirteen- to seventeen-year-olds in Bethesda, Maryland, work on the show A Chorus Line, a musical about the stress and triumph involved in trying out for a musical!*

Dance Vocabulary

Through the centuries many special words and phrases have developed to describe the movements, equipment, and jobs associated with dance. In ballet, many vocabulary words are in French, a tradition that began at the royal court in seventeenth-century France.

GRAND JETÉ

Grand jeté means "big jump," and that's just what Sheryl Ware, a New York City Ballet principal dancer, is doing here. During a *grand jeté,* a dancer leaps from one leg to the other, with legs outstretched. Before trying a jump like this one, dancers must build up their muscle strength and resilience. Ballet jumps look easy, but they are physically very demanding.

PAS DE DEUX

Pas means "step," and *deux* means "two." In ballet, a *pas de deux* is a dance for two people—it's a partnership. During a *pas de deux,* dancers use their strength to lift and support their partners, including moving them through the air. A *pas de deux* takes concentration and power yet must look graceful and light, as these Joffrey Ballet dancers, Valerie Madonia and Daniel Baudendistel, do.

CHOREOGRAPHER

The inventor of a dance piece is called a choreographer. Here, American choreographer Jerome Robbins holds one of his numerous awards. Robbins started out as a dancer and then became a choreographer for the American Ballet Theatre and the New York City Ballet. He choreographed many famous pieces, including "Fancy Free" and the dances in the musicals *West Side Story* and *The King and I.*

DANCE NOTATION

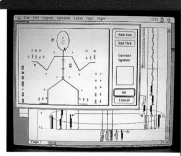

How do you write down the complex system of movements in a dance piece? Through dance notation. Several systems are in use. Some rely on symbols that stand for specific movements or body positions. Recently computer imaging has been used for dance notation. This system, called the Laban Method, is being used by choreographers and students nationwide.

FIRST POSITION

There are five basic positions for the feet in ballet. This is first position, in which the heels touch and the legs are turned out from the hip. One of the five foot positions is used at the beginning and end of each ballet movement. If you study ballet, these positions are the first thing you learn, because they are the foundation for everything else.

LEG WARMERS

Rummage in any dancer's bag of equipment, and you'll find some leg warmers bundled inside. Often hand-knit of wool, leg warmers help keep exercised muscles from cramping between warm-up and performance time. Dancers wear leg warmers as they wait to begin a performance. The fuzzy tubes will soon be stripped off and left backstage.

TOE SHOES

Also called *pointe* shoes, toe shoes are used for dancing on the tips of the toes. Ballerinas first used them in the nineteenth century. The tips are made of layers of cloth and glue built up into a solid block. Ribbons laced around the ankles hold the shoes on. Toe shoes must be gradually broken in to fit a dancer's foot. That takes time. But just one performance can be enough to wear a pair out!

TUTU

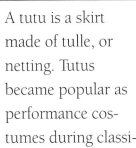

A tutu is a skirt made of tulle, or netting. Tutus became popular as performance costumes during classical ballet's romantic era, in the 1800s. The skirts can be long and graceful, or short and starched like the one in this photo. Short tutus show off complex leg movements in a ballet; longer, drifting ones emphasize graceful, flowing movements.

LEOTARDS AND TIGHTS

Both male and female dancers wear stretchy bodysuits called leotards and stockings called tights during practice and often during performances. They allow a dancer's body to move freely in all directions. They also allow dance teachers to see exactly how a dancer is holding his or her body and how the muscles are working.

TAP SHOES

Tap dancer Bill Robinson hugs his special tap shoes. The metal taps on toe and heel provide a dancer's own percussion section! Tap dance developed in the United States. It enjoyed a rage in the 1920s and remains popular today. In 1996, for example, Broadway audiences flocked to see tap dancing in the hit show *Bring in 'Da Noise, Bring in 'Da Funk*.

Dance around the World

At any time, day or night, somewhere in the world people are dancing. As you read these words, people are dancing. As you fall asleep tonight, someone somewhere will be dancing. Dance is an art that circles the world. These pictures celebrate dance styles of different cultures and places. In Seoul, South Korea, young dancers study for many years the traditional fan dance as shown in the large photo (left) at the Seoul High School of Music and Art. In Russia, ballet dancers—members of the world-famous Kirov Ballet company, which was founded in 1738—perform a perfect classical *pas de deux* in the ballet *Swan Lake* (above).

If you travel in another country, attend a dance performance. You will learn a lot about the spirit and history of the local people when you see them doing folk and ethnic dances that are hundreds of years old. These dances also help preserve traditional cultures. In Bangkok, Thailand, for example (below, far left), temple dancers give thanks to their gods in a ritual that has not changed for centuries; every movement has meaning. In the mountains of Colombia, South America, a couple dances outdoors to the rhythm of cumbia music and drums (below, second from left). In India, Kathakali dancers in elaborate costumes act out ancient tales through song and dance (below left). In Tbilisi, Georgia—part of the former Soviet Union—a children's folk dance group practices an exuberant dance in front of an old monastery (below right).

Dancing in Everyday Life

Has something important happened? Has a holiday arrived? Then it's time to dance! Dancing means celebration. At left, dragon dancers in the streets of Bali, Indonesia, welcome the new year.

In the large photo, samba dancers in feathered headdresses and sequined costumes dance in a parade during the annual celebration of Carnival in Rio de Janeiro, Brazil.

Dance often has religious meaning: People dance to worship. At far right, top, a young monk in Korea performs a butterfly dance at a funeral in a Buddhist temple. Dance commemorates life's other big moments, too: At a wedding in Cairo, women dance with candles on their heads to bring luck—and many children—to the bridal couple (far right, middle). In Africa, members of a Masai tribe leap straight into the air to honor the birth of a baby (far right, bottom).

Social dancing, such as the lively American country-western line dance like this one in Los Angeles (right), can be a great way for friends to have fun together—and get some exercise at the same time. Social dancing can also be a way for people to express their feelings for each other.

The World of Ballroom Dancing

During Christmastime in Washington, D.C., elegant couples, such as the one above, dressed in glittering gowns and formal tailcoats gather at a hotel for a ballroom dance competition. It's fun—but it's also *very* competitive. In these pictures, professionals and amateurs, including high school–age "junior" dancers, compete for bronze, silver, and gold medals in various dance rhythm categories, such as waltzes, fox-trots, and cha-chas. The dance competition lasts for three days, ending with the annual Yuletide Ball on New Year's Eve.

Ballroom dancing developed from popular European social dances, such as the waltz and the polka, and South American dances, such as the tango. In the 1910s the dance team of Vernon and Irene Castle adapted ballroom dancing for the stage and invented new social dances for couples. Their shows and dance styles made ballroom dancing all the rage! In the 1930s Fred Astaire and Ginger Rogers followed, making ballroom dancing look graceful, romantic, and effortless on the movie screen. People flocked to dancing schools to see if they could learn to dance like Fred and Ginger.

Ballroom dancing remains very popular all over the world. Ballroom dancers who compete, like those on these pages, follow rules and standards established by a large professional organization. Ballroom dancing is even a hit on college campuses, where young adults are learning the waltz, the swing, the jitterbug, and the fox-trot— dances their grandparents and even great-grandparents used to do.

At the Yuletide Ball in Washington, D.C., ballroom dance competitors Dan Callaway and Liana Turner (above) twirl and drag gracefully in a pasodoble for the judges. But before dancing, it's time to get ready by stretching (left). At far left, Pat Policella makes sure that college student and competitor Ntobeko Ntusi's bow tie fits perfectly. Ntobeko, who is from South Africa, studies ballroom dancing in Philadelphia and participates in many dance competitions in the United States.

High-tech Dance

Dance is an ancient art, but dancers, directors, and choreographers continue to transform it with new movements, modern materials, techniques, and equipment. They invent new costumes, like the otherworldly Triadic Ballet outfit (above). They create space-age effects with far-out stage sets and light and sound, as the Alwin Nikolais Dance Company does at right in the dance number *Circle and the Sphere*. Alwin Nikolais, known as Nik, invented total environments, not just dance movements, for his company. He began his career as a puppeteer but welcomed new technology. He was one of the first choreographers to use synthesized music. Another innovator, Merce Cunningham (inset, near right)—who has had a huge influence on modern dance since the 1950s—also connects technology and dance. He uses a complex computer notation program called Lifeforms to document his work. Computers are now becoming more common for coding dance pieces. One of the best-known programs, the Laban Method, is being used at Ohio State University by a graduate student to record movements made during a dance rehearsal (inset, far right).

Who will experiment with dance and technology in the twenty-first century? It could be you.

The History of Dance

If you could travel back in time, you would find dancers wherever you went. Their dance styles might seem familiar—or totally strange. Over time, dance has maintained many traditions and experimented with forms that never caught on.

On these pages are images of dancing people from many centuries. The dancer on the ancient Greek urn (above) is being honored with a wreath. At right, a painting by Pieter Brueghel the Younger, who lived from 1564–1638, captures the lively style of peasants celebrating at a wedding.

Dance delighted peasants, as well as the aristocracy. Ballet began in Italy, but it became a more formal art at the court of French king Louis XIV in the late 1600s. King Louis XIV established the Académie Royale de Danse, the first professional training school for ballet. The two drawings at right show what ballet looked like in his day and that of his successor, Louis XV.

In the 1830s the romantic era in ballet began, and dances choreographed then are still performed today. In 1832, Maria Taglioni performed *La Sylphide*, a ballet that tells the story of a fairy's tragic love for a human being. As La Sylphide, this Italian dancer changed ballet forever by dancing on the tips of her toes. Taglioni created this new, physically demanding style

In a sixteenth-century Flemish painting (top), peasants dance at a country wedding. At the French courts of Louis XIV (middle left) and Louis XV (middle right), costumes and manners were more formal. Formality reigned as a nineteenth-century pair waltzed at an inaugural ball (right).

shown above (second from left) in her performance of *La Bayadère* that is still used today. She also brought female dancers into the spotlight.

Russian ballet dancers such as Nijinsky (above left) and George Balanchine (above, far right) were also influential in making dance an important art form. Nijinsky danced with the Ballets Russes in Paris, while George Balanchine—who was both a dancer and choreographer—moved to America in 1933, where he founded a company that would grow into the very influential New York City Ballet. Another important company, the American Ballet Theatre, became the artistic home of such stars as Natalia Makarova, shown here dancing a traditional *pas de deux* from *Giselle* with Erik Bruhn (middle right).

Another Russian dancer who left his country and who is considered one of the most talented dancers of all time, Mikhail Baryshnikov (bottom right), trained in classical ballet tradition but has performed in many styles, including jazz and modern.

The Russian dancer Nijinsky became a phenomenal star when he danced with the Ballets Russes in Paris early in this century (above left). He traveled to Paris with another Russian, Serge Diaghilev (above, second from right), who was an impresario—a producer, organizer, and promoter of ballet. He hired dancers and choreographers who would go on to become famous, including George Balanchine (above, far right).

These three women—Isadora Duncan (above left), Doris Humphrey (above), and Martha Graham (left)—created a twentieth-century dance style that showed free-flowing body movements and emotions: modern dance.

José Limón and his partner (above) are a perfect example of the athleticism, freedom, and emotion of modern dance. In the 1950s Limón was one of dance's most influential choreographers.

Modern dance was born when Isadora Duncan, at far left, decided that dance should express the innermost feelings of humans. She inaugurated modern dance during the first year of the twentieth century with a performance of this new style in London. People were shocked, but Duncan went on to become a sensation. She danced barefoot and in flowing robes to the music of famous composers. Her daring, liberated style changed the way artists saw the body and reshaped their ideas of what was beautiful. The pictures at left show a gallery of other famous and creative modern dancers who followed Isadora Duncan and continued inventing new forms of movement.

Martha Graham created a personal, emotional style of modern dance. Her company became a training ground for generations of dancers and choreographers. She commissioned young composers to create music for her dances, including Aaron Copland's famous "Appalachian Spring," written in 1944. Graham was still performing into her seventies and died in 1991 at age ninety-two, one of dance's most famous figures.

Popular dance, such as tap and ballroom dancing, has also evolved during the twentieth century. The elegant Fred Astaire and Ginger Rogers (facing page, top center), brought ballroom dance to the screen in the 1930s—and into thousands of people's lives. Arthur Murray, shown doing the Charleston (facing page, top left), figured out that people needed help learning the different dances, and he made a fortune

by founding a chain of dancing schools that continue under his name today.

In the 1940s ballroom dance styles included the swing, stylishly executed by a young couple at top right. These dance forms grew up out of the culture of everyday life, but stars brought them to stage and screen. Brothers Maurice and Gregory Hines, at right, brought tap dancing back to Broadway; here they're performing in the smash hit *Sophisticated Ladies* in 1982.

If you want to see exciting new dance styles today, just turn on the television. Rock videos produced by such celebrities as Madonna, Janet Jackson, and Paula Abdul have generated a whole new wave of dance crazes that catch on almost overnight. That's superstar Michael Jackson performing (bottom right). Not only has his singing influenced cultures all over the world but so has his innovative choreography.

If you choose to become a dancer, you will find that the history of dance is full of stories of tradition and of innovation. When you have learned the dances of the past, you can let loose and create the dances of the future.

Shall we dance? *Popular dances of the twentieth century have included (from top left) the Charleston, the soft-shoe, swing, tap, and rock-and-roll extravaganzas on MTV. What will the twenty-first century bring?*

Other Famous Contributors

The "honor roll" of famous dancers is long—much too long to fit on these two pages! The portraits included here show some of the most influential dancers of the twentieth century. If you become a professional dancer, maybe your name will be added to a list like this some day.

ANNA PAVLOVA

This Russian ballerina, shown with one of her beloved pet swans wrapped around her neck, lived from 1882 to 1931. Pavlova was a global superstar. She performed worldwide, including in Japan and India, and was greeted by huge audiences wherever she went. Pavlova was probably best known for her short, heartrending signature dance, "The Dying Swan." She said that dance existed to give people "a sight of an unreal world, [as] beautiful [and] dazzling as their dreams."

BILL ROBINSON

An innovator in American tap dance, Bill "Bojangles" Robinson added a second tap to his shoes in the early 1920s. This improvement allowed tap dancers to add toe steps to the flat-footed movements they had used before.

GENE KELLY

Known for his acrobatic combinations of ballet, jazz, and tap, Kelly danced into America's heart in movies, including *On the Town* and *An American in Paris*. He's also famous for stomping in puddles as he performed the title song in the movie *Singin' in the Rain*.

NORA KAYE

Famous for her work in ballets that Antony Tudor choreographed for the American Ballet Theatre in the 1940s, Kaye was a great actress and dancer. Tudor's ballets were known for focusing on psychology and character as well as movement—a technique Kaye perfected.

AGNES DE MILLE

This dancer and choreographer is remembered for adding aspects of popular American dance styles to classical ballet. De Mille loved the American West. She choreographed *Rodeo*, a ballet, in 1942, and the dances for the Broadway musical *Oklahoma!*

ARTHUR MITCHELL
A dancer, choreographer, and educator, Mitchell formed Dance Theatre of Harlem in 1968. His many awards include a Mac-Arthur Foundation Fellowship, a Kennedy Center Honor, and fourteen honorary doctorate degrees.

DAME MARGOT FONTEYN and RUDOLF NUREYEV
One of the most famous ballet partnerships of all time began when Fonteyn was more than forty years old and about to retire from the Royal Ballet in London. The youthful Nureyev's fiery Russian style and Fonteyn's cool English reserve were a combination audiences loved, especially when they danced *Romeo and Juliet*, for which the pair often received flowers from enthusiastic fans.

ALVIN AILEY
As dancer, choreographer, and artistic director of the first African American dance company, which he founded in 1958, Ailey brought dance to a broader audience with such jazz and blues compositions as *Blues Suite* and *Revelations*.

JUDITH JAMISON
One of the best-known African American dancers, Jamison was a member of Alvin Ailey's company, for which she is now artistic director. Ailey choreographed a solo work, *Cry*, especially for her.

KATHERINE DUNHAM
After a successful career as a dancer in Chicago and New York, Dunham founded her own school in 1944 to formally train African American dancers in jazz dancing techniques.

TWYLA THARP
The innovative Tharp choreographed and danced the athletic *Push Comes to Shove* for the American Ballet Theatre, and she choreographed the dance scenes for the movie *Hair*.

CHITA RIVERA
This Hispanic American entertainer originated the Broadway role of Anita in *West Side Story* in 1957. Decades later she was still getting rave reviews for her performance in *Kiss of the Spider Woman*.

You Can Be a Dancer!

Merce Cunningham, the modern dance pioneer, has written: "Dance is of course for everyone to do. . . ." This means you!

You could decide to pursue the disciplined life of a classical ballet dancer or go wild with rock and roll. You could find a partner and compete as a ballroom dancer, or you could invent choreography that no one has ever thought of before. You could spend the summer learning to do a soft-shoe dance and belt out a Broadway tune. You could be a lighting technician or a costume designer. And you could be a star.

Reading is a good way to find out more about dance, but seeing live performances is even better. Dance is, after all, about bodies in motion. The photograph at left captures much of the energy and passion of young Spanish girls doing a flamenco in Madrid. Imagine seeing them in action!

Check your television schedule for shows about dance; consult the arts listings in the newspaper for information about performances by regional or national companies; attend street festivals and folk dance conventions. When you get home from your explorations in the world of dance, turn on some music and try some steps yourself.

Other Sources of Information

ASSOCIATIONS:

American Dance Guild
31 West 21st Street
New York, NY 10010

This group promotes dance nationally, produces a newsletter, and runs an annual conference.

American Dance Therapy Association
2000 Century Plaza, Suite 108
10632 Little Patuxent Parkway
Columbia, MD 21044-3263

A professional association for dance therapists, founded in 1966.

Dance/USA
1156 15th Street NW, Suite 820
Washington, DC 20005

National organization for professional dance in the United States.

Harlem Dance Foundation
American Dance Legacy Institute
144 West 121st Street
New York, NY 10027

A national educational organization that promotes the legacy of modern dance to children kindergarten age on up. Will provide curated video catalogs, repertory workshops, and tools for teachers and parents.

National Dance Council of America
824 St. Marks Avenue
Westfield, NJ 07090

An educational organization that provides information on professional dance and teaching groups, competi-

tions, and consumer brochures on such topics as choosing your performing arts school and choosing your ballroom instructor.

National Dance Association
1900 Association Drive
Reston, VA 22091

A national association for dance education that relates to health, physical education, recreation, and dance.

United States Amateur Ballroom Dancers Association Inc.
P.O. Box 128
New Freedom, PA 17349

Will refer public to one of 110 chapters for information on amateur ballroom events in local communities nationwide.

International Tap Association
P.O. Box 356
Boulder, CO 80306

Promotes development and preservation of tap dance as an art form. Offers a newsletter and information about tap dancing and related events around the world.

FESTIVALS:

American Dance Festival
(June–July)
P.O. Box 90772
Durham, NC 27708-0772

Colorado Dance Festival
(June–July)
P.O. Box 356
Boulder, CO 80306

Jacob's Pillow Dance Festival
(June–August)
Box 287
Lee, MA 01238

San Francisco Ethnic Dance Festival
Fort Mason Center
Landmark Bldg. D
San Francisco, CA 94123

Usually held in June for three weekends. Also affiliated with educational ethnic dance and music program for children called "People Like Me."

SCHOOLS OF DANCE:

The following ballet companies run schools for young dancers. Write to them to find out about applications and admission requirements, auditions, summer programs, etc. This is a selective list, not a comprehensive one. Check your local directory for schools of dance in your area.

School of American Ballet
70 Lincoln Center Plaza
New York, NY 10023-6592

Alvin Ailey American Dance Theatre
211 West 61st Street, 3d Floor
New York, NY 10023

Dance Theatre of Harlem
247 West 30th Street
New York, NY 10001

The Joffrey Ballet School
434 6th Avenue, 3d Floor
New York, NY 10011

San Francisco Ballet School
455 Franklin Street
San Francisco, CA 94102

The Washington Ballet
3515 Wisconsin Avenue NW
Washington, DC 20016

**Martha Graham School
of Contemporary Dance
Children and Teens Program**
316 East 63d Street
New York, NY 10021

*Offers a special youth dance
program in the fall from September
to December.*

National Dance Institute
594 Broadway, Room 805
New York, NY 10012

**MAGAZINES AND
REFERENCE SOURCES:**

Dance Chronicle
P.O. Box 331
Village Station, NY 10014

Published three times a year.

DANCE Magazine
33 West 60th Street
New York, NY 10023

Published monthly.

Dance Teacher Now
P.O. Box 41204
Raleigh, NC 27629

*A monthly magazine for dance teach-
ers that offers information on dance
classes, events, and competitions.*

**Dance Collection
New York Public Library for the
Performing Arts**
40 Lincoln Center Plaza
New York, NY 10023-7498

*One of the world's largest research
libraries for reference material on
dance. Houses a large archive on
children and dance.*

National Square Dance Directory
Box 880
Brandon, MS 39043

*Published once yearly. Includes all
national and local information related
to square dancing.*

Stern's Performing Arts Directory
33 West 60th Street, 10th floor
New York, NY 10023

PHOTO CREDITS